How to Write and Teach Case Studies Effectively?

KISHOLOY ROY
MBA, PGDAM, AMT, PhD (Pursuing)

Preface

It is a known fact that case based teaching has always been found to facilitate two way learning in class and have contributed to the healthy development of future professionals for it is one tool that makes student apply, think and come out with solutions and appreciate situations.

However for all this to happen there are two important ingredients to satisfy. One the case study itself. That is the quality of its development, the amount of research that has gone into its making and the way the case study has been presented. Case studies which are not engaging the target audiences can never be acceptable cases.

The second important aspect is at the delivery point where teachers come into the picture. How is a case being delivered to students? How are they being administered a case study? What sort of facilitation is being offered by the faculty? These all have a bearing on the quality of learning through cases.

This book deals with all these in three sections in a vivid and lucid manner. Also there are number of examples cited plus sample cases and other research materials given to explain the differences that exist in each of them.

Hope this effort from the author will definitely bring forth positive results in the context of case based education in the country. The cases mentioned in this books are from the marketing stream of management only.

Individuals who are interested to know about the nuances of case writing and develop themselves as good case writers and teachers who wish to have the right approach to case based teaching in classes will find this book extremely useful.

For queries/clarifications regarding any content in this book, one can get in touch with the author at scon60@gmail.com

KISHOLOY ROY

CONTENTS

(A)

Introducing Case Studies

What is a Case Study?

The most important question raised in this book perhaps for I have seen a number of people in the last 10 years who are unable to differentiate between a case study, and an article. They are confused to identify the difference either as content developers or as teachers imparting case study-based education. There is another content format that closely resembles case studies and they are caselets that have a bit different format. They explain/ inform what they have to in a short and precise manner and are devoid of certain structural formalities to be abided by case writers for case studies. Usually they are of a page or less than a page or can even exceed one page. They are often encountered by students during examinations of various subjects. A sample caselet can be found in **Annexure-II** at the end of this book.

A case study is defined as a description of an actual situation involving a challenge, opportunity, decision or problem faced by a decision maker. A case study is a story, a vehicle for discussion, analysis and learning. Case studies are meant to achieve certain teaching objectives and they comprise information and data that were available to the case developer at the time of the case development.

Case-based method of teaching originated at the Harvard Law School. Over the years there have been many universities and academic institutions that have prominently figured as potent sources of case study development. Harvard University, INSEAD internationally and Icfai University, Nirma University and Amity University in India have been found to develop case studies on various topics.

One of the biggest differences that lie between cases developed in India and those abroad is that the case studies at Harvard and INSEAD are more field based whereas in India, we come across more case studies based on published sources or on secondary research activity. However organizations like Harvard India Research Centre and the case development centre at IIM Calcutta are some who are aggressively promoting the cause of field based case development in the country.

The case-based method of learning relies on three fundamental aspects viz. Writing, Teaching and Learning where case writing is the most fundamental activity **(Exhibit-I)**. A well written case can go miles in communicating its teaching objectives and facilitate the learning process immensely.

Exhibit-I
Case Method Requirements

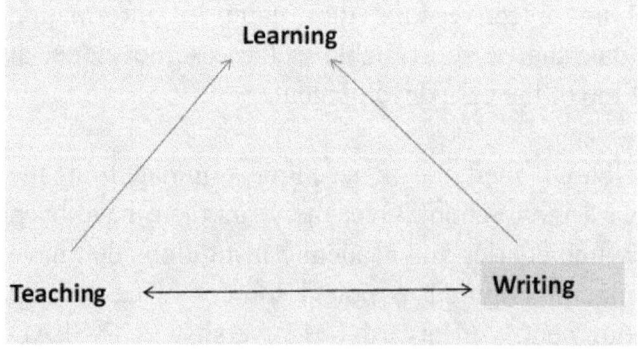

The creation and dissemination of knowledge through case studies has been regarded as a virtuous cycle by many as certain pertinent research questions help in the germination of a case study **(Exhibit-II).** Strong teaching objectives lay the foundation and then based on consultation with either the published sources or the empirical sources (the respondents), a case is developed and subsequently published.

Exhibit-II
The Virtuous Cycle of Case Development

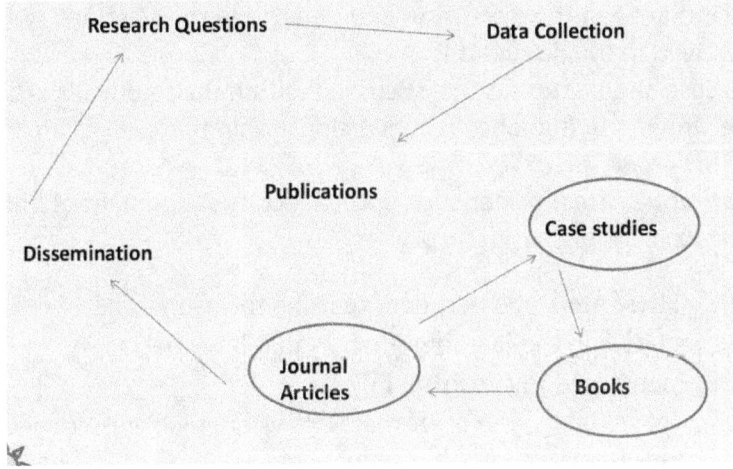

Case studies can be based on Business, Society and Government. On many occasions, a case can be found to present a convergence of all three or any two of the above mentioned domains. Themes of case studies can range from business and environment, health care, social enterprise, leadership and agri business. The timing of a case study is of immense importance as this can engage the audience and find maximum participation in its analysis. There are certain ingredients of a good case study as mentioned **in (Exhibit-III)**.

Exhibit-III
Ingredients of a Good Case Study

- should be relevant
- should present an opportunity to invite protagonist
- should establish a faculty as a specialist in the eyes of students
- should be tailor made to fit the requirements of an academic curriculum
- should have the cope of being amended based on class feedback or changes in environment
- should initiate healthy discussion and debates in the class and tempt everyone to be involved in the discussion
- a good case should not just be discussed within the four walls of a class but also after the target audience is conversing within themselves after the end of class
- the worth of a case also depends upon a faculty's judgment of bringing a particular case for discussion in class

There are some pertinent reasons for using case studies in the learning process that have been mentioned in **(Exhibit-IV)**.

Exhibit-IV
Why Use Case Studies?

- utilize theory, concepts, tools and techniques
- develop data, interpretation and analysis skills
- apply decision making skills
- practice interpersonal and communication skills
- create positive learning environment
- simulate reality
- learn by doing and by teaching others

Types of Case Studies

The case study types can be classified based on triggers involved, approach to development and the target audience for a case study. The case study types are mentioned in **(Exhibit-V).**

Exhibit –V
Types of Case Studies

• Based On Triggers Involved:
❑ Story driven cases – based on newspaper report, magazines etc
❑ Concept driven cases – based on a theoretical concept

• Based on Approach to development:
❑ Field research
❑ Secondary research

• Based on Target audience:
❑ For MBAs, BBAs – 12 -15 page case studies
❑ For Business executives – 3-6 pages condensed case studies
❑ For subject specific executive education – writing on a company
❑ For recruitment – for various academic programs. Very short cases.

There might be a case based on first mover disadvantage or on blue ocean strategy which will be a concept driven case while we come across many cases like McDonald's localization efforts across countries of the globe which will be triggered by some newspaper or magazine articles. The European Case Clearing House or ECCH now rechristened as *thecasecentre.org* is one of the largest repository of case studies in the world and there one will find all types of case studies listed above.

The Structure of Case Studies

Coming back to the most important and the very first question raised in this book which is what is a case study and how can you differentiate it from articles or technical or research notes?

Appendix I, II and III will give a clear idea regarding the differences that exist between a case, caselet, and an article. For now, it suffices to understand the fact that case studies are a dispassionate commentary being offered by the case writer about a company, a personality, a concept or a situation as the case may be. As a case writer one needs to have objectivity in place and should not be subjective or opinionated in their approach to writing else it becomes an article where an author is free to observe and comment in an engaging manner on a subject. A research article includes an empirical study about some aspect and then presenting the findings of the research work that may or may not support the literature study that forms the basis of any research article.

One has often come across two more products associated with case studies and they are a structured assignment and a teaching note. A structured assignment is meant for the students who will go through the case study and will then start working on the analysis by responding to the questions and guidelines as laid down in the structured assignment which consists of a series of questions that are aimed to make a student think laterally about a subject and not merely turn a case study into a reading comprehension exercise. A teaching note is meant for the teachers who conduct and execute case study sessions in class. It provides them a guideline as how to progress with a case study in class and the way students can be made innovative with their thoughts to solve cases. It also includes the theoretical concepts that form the thought behind a case. Case writers are often asked to develop case studies as a package which will have a case, a structured assignment and a teaching note.

Certain legal forms are associated with case development and they need to be procured/ furnished by any organization that is into development of case studies. Some of the key legal forms are mentioned in **(Exhibit-VI).**

Exhibit-VI
Key Legal Forms
- confidentiality
- case release
- case writer contract
- translator/proof reader contract
- assignment of rights (faculty)
- declaration of originality
- copyright request forms

In the next section we will look at how to write case studies effectively….

(B)

Writing Case Studies

Why Write and Release Case Studies?

This is the second most important question I suppose being raised in this book. Although this section will be dealing with the approach, structuring/ designing of case studies and their testing, the very first thing that comes to mind is why is this at all needed? Why to write something like a case study and why to release it in published format? The answers to these are mentioned in **Exhibit-VII** and **Exhibit-VIII**.

Exhibit-VII
Why Write Cases?

- provide local materials to target audience

- develop own learning materials

- contact with practitioner/business environment

- achieve educational objectives

- stay connected with present developments in the industry

- connect to research initiatives

Exhibit-VIII Why Release Cases?

- assure academic honesty

- validate company information

- grant permission to use

- maintain practitioner/academic relationship

Of course there are certain incentives for the content development and teaching community due to case studies. The corresponding incentives have been mentioned in **Exhibit-IX** and **Exhibit-X**.

Exhibit-IX
Incentives for Case Writers
- money
- academic interest
- intellectually stimulating
- ambition to teach
- make use of free time

Exhibit-X
Incentives for a Teacher
- impact
- improve quality of teaching
- incentives from school
- links with academic research

It has already been mentioned in the first section of this book that cases are broadly of two types based on approach to development of a case study. There are cases developed through secondary research and then there are cases developed through field/ primary research. The later one is significantly more time consuming since one has to wait for approvals for proceeding at various stages of its development e.g. before starting to write a case, proceeding with its development, approvals for including certain primary facts and figures of a company and then getting the final nod that the case has been effectively developed and is ready for publication from a suitable and relevant authority.

Case studies based on secondary research consume lesser time since majority of the issues are related to the case writer once he/ she gets the nod from the authority in an organization for proceeding with a case study. The research abilities of the case writer, the ability to write in an engaging and cohesive way and bringing out the problems/issues in an objective manner and doing justice to the teaching objectives of a case are all in hands of a case writer.

Case Development Process
Let's look at the case development process for the two types of case studies mentioned above in **Exhibits XI** and **XII**.

Exhibit-XI
Case Development Process- Field Research

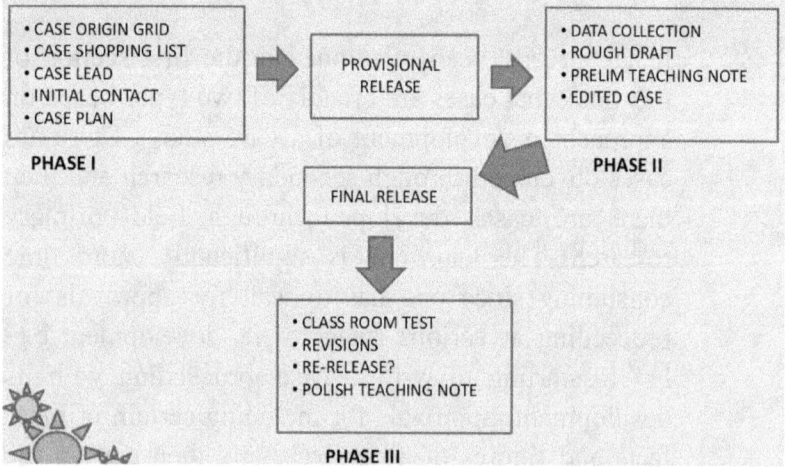

Exhibit-XII
Case Development Process- Secondary Research

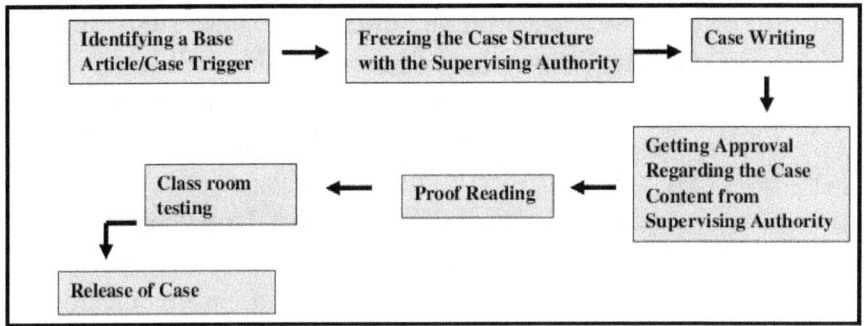

Proper planning of a case study is an extremely important activity to be performed in any case writing procedure. There are certain aspects of a case plan which have been mentioned in **Exhibit-XIII**.

Exhibit-XIII
Aspects of a Case Plan

• OPENING PARAGRAPH

• BRIEF STATEMENT OF TEACHING OBJECTIVES

• PROPOSED CASE OUTLINE BY SUBTITLES/SUBHEADS

• DATA REQUIREMENT LIST

• THE TIME PLAN

Whether it is a field research case or a case developed through secondary research, aspects of a case plan remain the same and the opening paragraph holds immense importance as far as the fate of a case study is concerned. The abstract of a case and the opening paragraph of a case study are the most important selling tools for a case. Improper choice of words or inability to define the crux of the case study and the selling proposition of the case study will leave a case to be unsold and unacceptable in the industry and thereby the very purpose of developing gets defeated. If you visit the *thecasecentre.org* site, you will find cases needed to be bought based on their abstracts and hence until and unless as a case writer, you come up with a compelling abstract to a case, your product will be left untouched, unvisited and UNSOLD. After all selling a case is the ultimate motive of any organization that is into case development for this is definitely not a charitable activity. So much of intellectual capital investment can not be afforded to go waste.

The opening paragraph of a case study is a crucial element of the case study. It tells the reader to take on the position of the person within the organization at a certain point of time, at a certain location and resolve the issue being mentioned in the case study. Case writers should ideally follow a check list for writing opening paragraph of case studies **(Exhibit-XIV)**. This will enable them to initiate cases effectively as writers.

Exhibit-XIV
Checklist for Opening Paragraph

- is the decision maker identified by name and position?
- is the time frame of the case study clear?
- is the location of the company identified?
- is the decision, issues, challenges, opportunities or problems clear?
- is the decision sufficiently interesting for use in class?
- is the story line cut appropriately? (What happened, To whom? When? Where? Why? How? What preceded? What followed?
- is the decision frame cut appropriately?
- what is the action trigger?
- is the case title appropriate?

With two sample opening paragraphs below, you can decide for yourself whether they conform to the standards of effective opening paragraph development or not:

Case Title:
Burnol: The Burns Specialist

Opening Para:
"In 2004, Jack Periera, Brand Manager for Burnol in Dr. Morepen tried to find a viable solution to revive brand Burnol before his meeting with Karthik Raina, Managing Director, Dr. Morepen. The product Burnol was acquired by Dr. Morepen, a fully owned subsidiary of Morepen Laboratories Ltd. In 2002 from Reckitt Piramal. It is one of the rare cases where India's leading brand has changed hands. Dr. Morepen is the brands' third owner, and it bought the brand for INR 8.5 crores. However, this constant change over of this brand from one company to another has virtually undermined the equity of this heritage brand."

NOW DOES THIS OPENING PARAGRAPH CONFORM TO THE CHECKLIST?????

Case Title:
Café Coffee Day: Brewing a Brand in a Different Way

Opening Para:
"Siddhartha, Chairman of Café Coffee Day, was sitting in office with a cup of coffee in his hand reading the newspaper, focusing particularly on the article that read, "Starbucks planning its entry into India." With Lavanza already as the owner of both Barista and Fresh and Honest coffee brands, he could not help contemplating the changing coffee retailing industry scene in India"

NOW DOES THIS OPENING PARAGRAPH CONFORM TO THE CHECKLIST?????

Staying with the issue of salability of cases, there are two more important aspects that define this parameter. One is the way teaching or pedagogical objectives are framed for the case and two the tags or keywords supplied for the case study. We all understand that online is the place where transactions are on the rise and hence for anyone to chance a look at your case, you need to supply such keywords that are broad based, relevant and give a clear indication as to the areas of a subject that your case study is dealing with.

Interviews happen to be a very important element of case development as far as field research based cases are concerned and hence one needs to understand how to approach this activity. **Exhibit-XV** mentions the same.

Exhibit-XV
Conducting Interviews for Case Development

1. Beginning
- ➢ thank contact person for agreeing to meet
- ➢ exchange business cards
- ➢ explain who you are, why you are there, what you would like, confidentiality (case not to be published until permission granted by the company official), disguise options

2. *Conducting*
- ➢ prioritizing case preferences
- ➢ ask decision oriented questions
- ➢ if 'no' is the answer to each question, ask what was the most challenging decision taken lately or what are the present issues facing the company

3. *Ending*
- ➢ thank contact person
- ➢Arrange a time to review the case plan

4. *Following*
- ➢ review and clarify notes for each case preference discussed

REMEMBER TO ALLOW 60-90 MNTS FOR INITIAL INTERVIEW

Identifying a Trigger for a Case

When it comes to developing cases based on secondary research or based on published sources, the activity of identifying a suitable trigger for the case is of paramount importance. A case trigger can also be mentioned as a base article for a case since it will be the content that will provide significant fodder for thought to the case writer and will serve as the foundation for the case. There are certain published sources that are more acceptable as sources for base articles of case studies. Publications like *The Economic Times, Financial Times, Business Standard, Fortune magazine, The Economist* are often scanned for seeking articles for writing cases.

However for me, identification of base article should definitely be related to a publication's brand name as this carries a certain stamp of assurance about its authenticity. But then, more important is the merit of the article being considered as base article. Case studies based on secondary research contains lots of quotes of various personalities from an industry or company and one should see to it that the base article has some real defining quotes in it. Often the opening quote of a case is taken from the base article. The base article should be such that it facilitates framing the structure of the case and gives me the case writer and the supervisor ample scope to appreciate the issues to be discussed in the case.

Once the base article or the case trigger is identified, one proceeds with finding further inputs to supplement the case and make it really engaging along with authentic facts and figures drawn from various sources. Yes, authenticity is one big issue and hence case writers are often discouraged to consult Wikipedia or for that matter any blog for facts and figures while writing cases because in the former case, it is a platform open to editing at any point of time by any user and in the later case, the blog may contain opinions of a person and not a dispassionate or transparent content which can disillusion a case writer.

Structure of a Case Study

A case study comprises of various elements that form the structure of a case and are integral to making it a winning and purposeful case. The elements are:

- ✓ The title of a case study
- ✓ Opening quote of a case study
- ✓ Opening paragraph/ introductory section of a case
- ✓ Company/ industry/ conceptual background
- ✓ Major issues that the case discusses
- ✓ Conclusion

Apart from the above, one needs to insert Exhibits and Tables wisely in a case and many times certain inputs are mentioned in the Annexure section mentioned at the end of a case. While diagrams and photos are mentioned as Exhibits in a case, figures are generally mentioned in Tables.

It is a good practice to offer footnotes for certain crucial and defining figures being mentioned in a case. Footnotes are to be mentioned for any quote being mentioned. **Annexure I** in this book will help you to understand what footnotes are and how they to be mentioned in a case. On many occasions, instead of footnotes, case writers are encouraged to go for endnotes at the end of a case. However the practice of giving footnotes is more acceptable. Times New Roman is the most acceptable font for writing cases and 12 is the most acceptable font size. Sources for every Exhibit and Table are to be mentioned below any such element within a case.

We will now look at each of the defining elements of a case that comprise a case structure.

To start with, let's look at the **Title of a case**. It is extremely important to go for a pertinent and witty title for a case since it is another very important element that can make or break the sale of a case. Cases are supposed to offer dilemma, raise questions and issues and debates and hence it is advisable to go for a title that has a question mark at the end. My first published case study was on McDonald's and incidentally I strongly believe that it was the title of the case which made it a really successful case in terms of sales. It was titled **McDonald's Localization Strategy: Brand Unification, Menu Diversification?** (**ECCH** *Reference Number: 306-316-4*). Now if you look at this title, you see that the title raises not just interest among readers with the choice of words but it also gives readers and prospective buyers what can they expect from the case study. This is one of the best practices of case writing. You keep your title as short and crisp as possible and give ample scope to reader to understand and gauge the canvas of your case study.

Next we look at the **Opening Quote** of a case. The opening quote sets the tone of a case and it is here that it can be differentiated from the other quotes a case writer puts within the text of the case. A case can have one opening quote that more or less summarizes the content of the case or it can have two opposite tones of quotes/opinions to clearly highlight the debate which is present within the case. Many years back, I have done a case study titled **Pope and**

Product Placements: Marketers' 'Holy' Connections and from there I present the opening quotes and you see for yourself how well the debate present within the case has been brought out through the opening quotes:

Being associated with the pope is worth at least 100 times more than an A-list celebrity because the pontiff has a more devoted following.[1]

– **John Allert**, *Chief Executive, Interbrand*[2] *(Britain)*

Pursuing pope-and-product juxtaposition poses risks. Brands have to be careful not to appear opportunistic or they could risk a backlash with the pope's admirers.[3]

I have already spoken at length about the opening paragraph and its significance and hence I am not going to delve deeper into it. Remember one thing that this opening paragraph is the window to your case and thus it is supposed to present the gist of the case in an engaging way. It must briefly contain all that your case has.

Regarding the remaining elements of a case study, you can take a look at **Annexure I** of this book to understand things in a better way. Also take a close look at footnote styling over there.

It is an important requirement that there is suitable connectivity between the various sections of a case study and to ensure that you need to have a sentence that does the job else it will look as if each section is an island and there is no integration or cohesiveness as such within a case. Over here, I present to you a case study I wrote on Harry Potter..the connecting sentences in each section are highlighted for you:

Section I: Introduction

Children's literature, that originated in the 17th century have been found to possess certain distinct characteristics. Some of the broadly defined and accepted characteristics include stories written and marketed for children, children playing the lead roles, the language of which is simple and includes illustrations. In the twentieth century, fairy tales, fantasies and illustrated books were found to assume popularity among children. The English literature presented children's fiction like Alice in Wonderland, Cinderella, Snow White and Seven Dwarfs et al. It was further observed that authors came up with sequels to some of the extremely successful children's stories like Famous Five, Nancy Drew and Hardy Boys. The Indian equivalent of which were Akbar Birbal, Vikram Betaal, Chacha Chaudhary and Thakumaar Jhuli (Bengali children's literature). However, these all were found to belong to that genre of children's literature that were initially innocent, subsequently oversold and eventually abandoned pre-teen obsessions. In the late 1990s, e-books and CD-ROMs of the above classics were released in the market to improve sales but such formats failed to generate sufficient sales. The need of the hour was to package a children's literary work in an attractive and appealing manner.

Section II: Breaking the Jinx

It was Harry Potter and the Philosopher's Stone by J.K. Rowling published by Bloomsbury in the UK in 1997 that was found to break the jinx as far as a children's literary work witnessing significant success is concerned. The Harry Potter series was about an orphan boy with magical powers. The series was planned by Rowling to comprise of seven parts, one for each of the seven years spent by Potter at the Hogwarts School of Witchcraft and Wizardry. The novels were supposed to deal with various adventures of Potter and introduce the readers to various friends (like

Ron Weasley and Hermione Granger) and enemies (like Lord Voldemort) of Potter......

.............To commemorate the success of the Harry Potter series, Royal Mail, the national postal service provider in the UK commissioned a set of stamps which feature the book covers of the seven books published by Bloomsbury.

Section III: The Merchandising Deals

In 1998, Warner Brothers Consumer Products, after realizing the huge potential that the Harry Potter books had for merchandising and movies, bought the worldwide film, licensing and merchandising rights for Harry Potter from J.K. Rowling for $5, 00,000....

Hope this above excerpt from my case on Potter has given you ample understanding regarding how to frame and execute connecting sentences that binds sections of a case study and is an effective tool for keeping readers engaged and keeping alive their interests in reading a case.

Case writers should be aware of the '75-25' principle while writing case studies. 75% of the length of the case study should be dedicated towards speaking about the issues, situations and dilemmas being raised in the case and 25% of the case length to be dedicated to supporting/ background information like the Background Study of a company or industry or concept and the Introduction of the case study.

Footnote Styling

Let's first look at footnote for the opening quote of a case study. The footnote for the opening quote should be mentioned just after the quote and not after the individual who mentioned the quote. The individual whose opening quote is given needs a description in brief in the footnote inserted after his name as the person's credibility needs to be established. An individual should be carrying sufficient importance or his/her designation should be carrying significance because of which the opinion of the individual has been mentioned in the opening quote of a case study.

It's a saga of the immigrant experience that captures the snap, crackle and pop of American life, along with the pounding pulse, emotional reticence, volcanic colors and cherished rituals of Indian culture.[1]

– Joe Morgenstern,[2] Film Critic, *The Wall Street Journal*

---

[1] Morgenstern Joe, "'Namesake' is a Richly Spiced Immigrant Saga", http://online.wsj.com/article/SB117339757711731537.html?mod=todays_asia_weekend_journal, March 9, 2007.

[2] Joe Morgenstern is a movie critic with *The Wall Street Journal.* He was awarded the 2005 *Pulitzer Prize* for his reviews on films released in the year 2004.

Hope the above example gives a clear understanding as how to go about mentioning footnotes for the opening quotes of a case study.

While mentioning footnotes for the exhibits in a case study, one should follow the following style:

Source: Author's Name (of the article from where the exhibit has been taken; surname first followed by the first name of the author), the title of the article (which is to be mentioned within double quotes), the source of the article like www.******.com/org/in or *The Times of India* (offline sources to be mentioned in italics), date of the article

In case the exhibit is created by the author of the case study, it should be mentioned *Compiled by the author*.

While mentioning footnotes two consecutive references taken from the same source is mentioned as Ibid (when the source is to be quoted for the second consecutive time in the same page). If a reference has already appeared before but not exactly the previous one, mention the footnote as "Article name", op.cit.

Given below are some sample footnotes for better understanding:

Let's say that there is an article by an author named Anna Bilel in the Businessworld magazine dated 10th March 2006 titled The Extinction of the Jaguar, the footnote styling will be:

Bilel Anna, "The Extinction of the Jaguar", *Businessworld*, March 10th 2006

In case of online sources, the complete URL of the source is to be mentioned in the footnote after the title of the article is mentioned.

In case of two authors, the authors are to be mentioned in the footnotes as Surname of first author followed by the first name of the first author and similarly the second author is to be mentioned. Here is an example: Seal Adam and Kolt Paul

If there are more than two authors for an article, one need to mention just the first author (surname followed by first name) and then mention et.al as mentioned here: Seal Adam et.al.

Editing Case Studies

Once the case leaves the case writer's table, it comes to the case editor or the content editor or the supervisor; you may call the person whatever you like to. However the fact is this is the person who evaluates the quality of a case, pin points the errors made by the case writer and offer suggestions to him/her for improving the output. He is also the person who is supposed to do the plagiarism check whenever and wherever he is in doubt. A case editor too has a checklist of things to do and check out in a case which are mentioned as the 9Cs of case editing **(Exhibit-XVI)**. Remember proper case studies do not carry assignment questions along with them. Over here, by proper I mean properly structured case studies and am not hinting at content of a case.

Exhibit-XVI
9Cs of Case Editing

- **Congruence**: case language vs company data and terminology
- **Completeness**: story line gaps, omissions
- **Consistency**: story line logic and accuracy, beginning and ending time, decision frame and the disguise used throughout
- **Correctness**: tense, spelling, grammar, exhibit presentation, referencing, attributions (unlike opinions, they are case facets as reported/found in the organization)
- **Clarity**: precise words, language
- **Control**: headings, paragraphs, logical grouping
- **Coherence**: linking, connecting, ideas
- **Conventions**: title page, formatting, referencing, reprinting, abbreviations, copyright statement, NO ASSIGNMENT QUESTION IN THE CASE

Once the case editor goes through a case, he/she will be sending it back to the case writer for the suggested changes to be incorporated. Until and unless a case study gets the approval of the supervisor and proof reader, it is regarded as a draft and hence there is something called the first draft, second draft of the case study depending on how many times it is moving to and fro from the writer's to the editor's table. Once a case gets approval of the case editor, it is sent to a proof reader for identifying certain grammatical errors, errors of punctuation etc. and again these needs to be incorporated by the case writer.

Classroom Testing

With all suggestions incorporated to the satisfaction of authorities by the case writer, the case study now stands approved and is ready for class testing to establish its feasibility and relevance in a class. There may be occasions when due to unsatisfactory performance of a case in a class, it may well go back to case writer's table for further improvisation.

Whether a case study serves its relevance and purpose or not can be understood by the answers to certain key questions mentioned in (**Exhibit-XVII**).

Exhibit-XVII
The Key Questions

• DOES THE CASE FULFILL/ACHIEVE TEACHING OBJECTIVES? "IS IT A GOOD CASE?"

• WOULD FURTHER CHANGES MAKE IT A BETTER CASE? (CHANGES TO INFORMATION PRESENTATION OF THE CASE STUDY)

• WOULD CHANGING THE CASE TEACHING PLAN PRODUCE A BETTER DISCUSSION?

• WHAT ANALYSIS/ COMMENTARY CAN BE ADDED TO THE TEACHING NOTE?

Classroom performance of a case study can sometimes turn out to be unsatisfactory as stated earlier and there can be several reasons for the same as mentioned in (**Exhibit-XVIII**).

Exhibit-XVIII

Reasons for Unsatisfactory Performance

- PROBABLY BECAUSE OF THE METHOD OF TEACHING

- ..... BECAUSE OF THE EQUIPMENTS OR FACILTIES AVAILABLE IN THE CLASS

- ..... BECAUSE OF THE PEOPLE INVOLVED (STUDENTS/ INSTRUCTOR)

- ...... BECAUSE OF THE MATERIAL/CONTENT OF THE CASE STUDY

Case Release

Once a case study clears the classroom test, it is ready for upload/publication for which certain legal formalities and documentation is required as mentioned earlier. *thecasecentre.org* requires an organization or an individual to furnish a document at the time of upload. This document requires one to fill up the name(s) of author(s) along with the title of the case study and the keywords for the case. One also needs to mention whether the case has been written using published sources or is it the output through field research. One also needs to mention whether the case has been tested in class or not and at what level and with how many students as audience. In conclusion as far as this section is concerned, we look back at the steps involved in case development through **(Exhibit XIX).**

Exhibit XIX
Case Development in a Nutshell

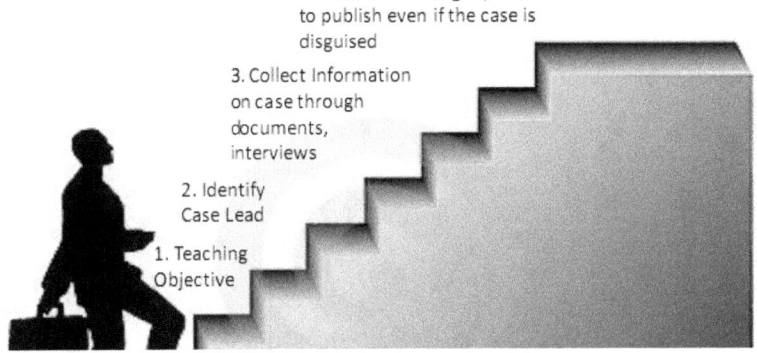

Balakrishnan (2010)

In the next section, we will take a look at how to teach case studies effectively…

(C)

Teaching Case Studies

Why Teach Cases?

This is perhaps the third and last crucial question raised in the book. Well, frankly and simply speaking, teaching cases is one of the most potent tool to trigger two way learning in class. As a teacher, you lecture, you show slides; the activity is more or less unilateral. The participation of the other side (that is the students) is almost insignificant. But then it is through case based teaching that you encourage wholesome participation and allow breeding of ideas in class.

Teaching Cases – What Cases to Teach?

As a faculty, you need to take a judicious call as to what cases you are bringing to class. In this part of the world, I have often found teachers bringing cases to class either to establish their conformance to western philosophy of teaching professional courses or to just while away time since they are incapable of taking full length lecture sessions due to lack of knowledge or incapability to counter questions posed by students while being taught a particular topic.

As a teacher, you need to understand the importance of what cases you are bringing to class. Situations can be pathetic if you offer an MBA level case study to BBA students or vice-versa. Selection of case studies should be based on content, their relevancy, their recency and finally how much participation can a case study encourage.

I have often found that teachers bring case studies that are published in a text book, a popular one which the faculty has either recommended or not recommended to students. This practice is not worthy for mostly a text book takes time to be called dated but such is not the case with a case study. A case study is often found to be based on a situation that existed when the book was written. Now if a case written some 5-10 years back is brought to class and students are asked to solve it, the amount of innovation from them that could have been commanded gets diluted. Teachers often practice this to put lesser effort to case based teaching. They often themselves do not go through a case in totality before bringing the same to class. The ideal way out is to leverage the power of the Internet which is nothing but a treasure house of knowledge and if well utilized and one knows the right way to search for information on the net, one can end up getting contemporary cases with the right content to stimulate students and trigger purposive action in them.

Teaching Cases – How to Teach Cases?
As mentioned in the earlier section, case study teaching is meant to involve students. It is meant to encourage and enhance student participation. It is a tool to boost the power among students to think laterally because until and unless that power gets developed a student in the long run cannot penetrate the gates of hallowed companies of this world. Bookish and mugged up knowledge cannot spell success for a student doing professional studies of any kind for these studies are meant to motivate a student to apply thoughts and apply them differently from scores of other people in the industry. Then only a person can be successful and looked up to in the business.

One aspect that I deliberately did not mention in the previous section is whether to bring such case studies to a class of MBA students that have questions at the end of case study or not? Well since this is concerned with the 'how to' part, I will speak about it here. For BBA students, considering their average age and the education life cycle, getting to solve cases with questions at the end might be an okay ploy although I am not totally in favor of that but this is certainly a 'no-no' in an MBA class of students. Case study analysis is not a reading comprehension exercise where everything is tailor made for you to understand and score. As a student, one needs to dissect a case, do a post-mortem of the situation being mentioned in the case and as the doctor who conducts the post-mortem you are supposed to unearth the real issue and subsequently come up with a solution for the same.

For purposes of class activity, after taking theoretical sessions on a subject/topic, administering case studies is a must and not caselets. As mentioned earlier in the book, caselets are fine for examination purposes and not for class teaching and that means you as a faculty are supposed to administer a content that is at least 3-7 pages long. Anything under 10 pages should be fine but then considering the attention span of students in contemporary times and the level of patience they carry, faculty interacting regularly with students must understand and administer cases ideally suited to the target audience. There are institutes where case studies of 15-25 pages are also administered but then I will consider them as exceptions in this part of the world.

Many times while scouting for case studies on the Internet, I have come across case studies that are 10 or more pages long. But then I find that the case has not adhered to the '75-25' principle which means there are far too many aspects mentioned in the case that are not central to the case study. I have deleted all such pages and brought the creamy part of the case study for analysis in class. This does two things. First you get the class to solve an issue in an area you want to and second you do some surgery to the case study so that it can fit the acceptance level of the target audience.

Case studies should be handed over to students for analysis in advance so that they have ample time before they are asked to make a class presentation on the same. Case study analysis to me should be a group activity where a group of 4-5 students ideally work together, do the brainstorming and come up with an appreciable analysis of the case study.

Now I have mentioned about doing post mortem to a case but then HOW? Well, I mentioned about structured assignments somewhere earlier in this book which consists of a series of analytical questions related to a case. Questions that make a person think and do not trigger straight answers. One has to research, go back and forth in the case study, do some additional readings to respond to the question. Students need to do that. WHY?

Well, first and foremost many a time, you do not get readymade structured assignments for case studies and so this activity makes sense. Second, this is the right way to analyze cases where you yourself identify potential issues in a case study and come up with solutions which go on to build the power to think laterally among students.

Another important thing is that you as a faculty have to work along with students of course at your own level. Merely asking students to develop questions is not enough until and unless you yourself develop few questions and put them to students to make students understand what sort of questions need to be developed so that they do a post-mortem of a case, so that they are called analytical questions, so that they stimulate lateral thinking and so that one feels the urge and the need to do supplementary studies to analyze a case. Yes this is very important as no case is developed in isolation and is actually built using various contents from here and there. To understand and appreciate the crux of a case or theoretical background of a case, further studies need to be done. A faculty thus needs to set examples in front of students and make them appreciate the fact that he is equally involved in the process of case analysis and is there with them as their mentor. Two way learning through case based education cannot take place with a teacher in class but only when that teacher dons the role of a mentor.

A sample case study that was administered in a class sometime back along with some analytical questions developed is mentioned below:

An Opportunity Ignored.
A Fortune Lost.

© Kisholoy Roy

Small opportunities are often the beginning of great enterprises.
-Demosthenes

The idea of 'Fortune at the Bottom of the Pyramid' was put forward by C K Prahlad in his book of the same name. The simple and novel idea proposes to regard the poor segment of the society as a potential consumer segment, thus opening up a whole new opportunity for entrepreneurship and prosperity. Here is a case study that exemplifies this philosophy and drives home the idea that in business, there is life beyond the bottom line.

First, let's take a look at the S-T-P analysis of the Indian jeanswear market and its leading players.

Market Segments Identified(based on pricing)	Premium, Semi-premium, Value
Market Segments Identified	Staple, Fashion, Value-add-ons
Target Markets	Teenagers and Youth
Various Criteria for Positioning	Price, Styling, Brand Personality, Product Durability
Leading Brands	Forever Jeans, O'ram Jeans, Thomas Hardy
Market Share Rankings	1. Forever Jeans 2. Thomas Hardy 3. O'ram Jeans

The above details present an overview of the S-T-P analysis executed by the various corporate entities in the Indian jeanswear market. It also highlights the present position of O'ram Jeans via-à-vis its competitors. O'ram Jeans as a brand is manufactured and marketed by US based H&C O'ram Inc., that entered India in 1992. The brand was considered a synonym for jeans and denim-wear worldwide and it enjoyed the highest recall among its target audience at that juncture.

In the early 1990s, the country's denim market was found to be largely unsegmented. Although jeans were popular with the youth in terms of their aspirational value, their demand was by and large being met by the unorganised sector. The only recognised jeanswear brand at that point of time was Forever Jeans -- a brand promoted by Ahmedabad-based Amber Textiles since 1990. Forever Jeans had a strong focus on the smaller towns of the country. Those were the places where people aspired to don jeans and wanted to imbibe international fashion trends but at affordable rates. Amber Textiles offered just that, plus its range of jeanswear was found to be extremely durable, both in terms of stitch and colour. This ensured that the jeans stayed in extremely good condition despite several washes. However, it was observed that there was little differentiation between men's and women's styles where jeanswear was concerned. O'ram Jeans was the first international brand to enter the Indian market and the one aspect that worked in its favour was that it was the most respected global brand at that point of time. It was reported, that globally O'ram Jeans positioned itself as a brand for the masses, but when it entered India, it positioned itself as a premium product, courtesy premium imagery and pricing (prices started at INR 1100). The positioning seemed to backfire at the outset to a certain extent, because though the brand's target customer base was in the 16 - 25 years age groups, who were open to international fashion, they were unable to pay for the price. The jeanswear market was more or less in its nascent stage and customers were not quite aware of the various functional and emotional aspects attached with jeanswear as a product category that contributed to their pricing. The retail consultants pointed out that the company's advertising and marketing strategies failed to explain why consumers needed to pay a premium for the brand. H&C O'ram Inc. was found to concentrate all its efforts on bottomwear. Topwears or denimwears for women and children did not figure in its strategy radar. The company began its Indian business sojourn by establishing 40-odd exclusive outlets across various metros of the country. Though the sales figure for O'ram Jeans seemed unsatisfactory in the eastern region, the brand did well in other parts of the country.

In 1995 and 1996, there were a couple of international brands that entered the Indian jeanswear arena. Prominent among those was Thomas Hardy, a brand manufactured and marketed by the US-based Morrison Group. The company was found to be straddling the semi-premium and premium segment of the market. The price for its product range was between INR 799 and INR 1299. The company was innovative, both in its product strategy and in brand communications. It promoted its jeans brand through endorsements by the leading young achievers of the country. The company's distribution strategy enabled Thomas Hardy to make radical inroads into the country's jeanswear market as it focused on metros as well as non-metros.

While O'ram Jeans ignored the idea of focusing on denimwears for children and women and topwears in general, Thomas Hardy emphasised those areas. Also, while Thomas Hardy focused on the design aspect of its product range, O'ram continued with its staple styling believing that the style will be loved for its retro look of the 1960s and 1970s. There was one huge difference between O'ram Jeans and the other prominent brands like Forever Jeans and Thomas Hardy. That was, while the other brands had sought a distinct position in the consumers' perceptual territory. O'ram Jeans failed to do so. It was further observed that though Forever Amber Textiles garnered less revenues from its per unit sales, it enjoyed market leadership, courtesy the number of units sold, while Thomas Hardy dislodged O'ram Jeans from the No.2 position in 1998 by innovating across markets.

In 2002, as a reactionary measure to its fast eroding market share, O'ram Jeans initiated the process of marketing jeanswear for ladies and children. But, by then, metro markets were saturated. H&C O'ram Inc. decided to adopt a different distribution strategy in order to seek more market penetration not only in the metros but to some extent in the other urban areas of the country. It joined hands with Oberoi Bros. -- a Delhi-based garment merchant that manufactured and distributed cotton and denimwear through its own chain of countrywide outlets. The product range of the company was generally perceived to be cheap and of inferior quality and, so, when O'ram Jeans tied up with Oberoi Bros. for distributing its premium range of jeanswear, it sent confusing signals to the market and in the process, its equity got further diluted.

In 2004, a leading market research agency of the country offered H&C O'ram Inc. certain measures that could arrest the decline in its market share. It was suggested that the company move to the smaller towns and certain rural areas where the concept of jeanswear was still new ,but the demand for denim wear existed and could be exploited to garner revenues, provided the company modified its product and pricing policies. There was scope for innovation over there, which was almost negligible in the existing markets. The top management in the company, however, dismissed the suggestions, stating several reasons. One with the current cost structures, the company could not profitably compete for that market. Secondly, people in the rural and smaller towns in India were not quite prepared to accept jeans as a dress code, both monetarily and attitude-wise. Thirdly, the suggested market was not viable for the long-term viability of the business. Finally, the managers in charge of strategic implementation would not derive intellectual excitement and they would not be interested in activities that would have more of a humanitarian dimension. On the other hand, the company would do well if it expanded its distribution network in a more prudent manner and tried to device ways of making the pricing more competitive in its existing markets.

However, such measures did not help the company's cause as the market share and the revenues kept declining. In 2006, its market share reached the nadir. The market share for various brands in 2006 was as follows: Forever Jeans: 57 %, Thomas Hardy: 23 %, O'ram Jeans: 11 %, Others: 9 %.

What could have been the various reasons for the continuous and radical decline in the sales and market share of O'ram Jeans? What should H&C O'ram Inc. have done to regain at least its lost ground and thus pose a tough challenge for its competitors in the days ahead?

****

Few Analytical Questions Developed based on the Case Study:

☐ *"Small opportunities…". Expand this idea based on rural marketing initiatives undertaken by companies in the last decade in India?*
☐ *Comment on the S-T-P analysis executed by companies mentioned in the case study for the Indian jeanswear market?*
☐ *Comment on the strategic fallacies of O"ram Jeans?*

☐ *What do you understand by the term „perceptual territory"? Create a mental map based on jeanswear marketers mentioned in the case?*

☐ *„Ineffective distribution strategy can lead to brand dilution". Support this idea based on the contents of this case study?*

Annexure I: CASE STUDY

Brand Motorola in India: Analyzing its Growth Strategies

In December 2007, Motorola announced the launch of its latest handset, MOTOYUVA W180 that was targeted at the Indian youth. After pursuing sub-branding strategies based on feature and function of the handsets, Motorola was found formulate its latest sub-branding strategy based on a particular target segment and that was youth. Speaking at the launch of the handset, Llyod Mathias, director marketing, mobile devices, Motorola, India and South West Asia observed, "The MOTOYUVA W180 seeks to address the needs of the aspiring Indian consumer for whom affordability and features are essential, without compromising on design and premium experience. W180's brilliant screen and robust features bring rich colors of Indian culture into your phone."[1]

However, it was 2006 that saw a turnaround in Motorola's fortunes in India. From being ranked fifth in terms of market share till 2005, Motorola climbed on to claim the No. 2 spot which it has zealously maintained since then. Experts opine that it was Motorola's strategy of going for catchy names for its sub-brands that enabled Brand Motorola to occupy a distinct position in the consumer's perceptual territory. Motorola's sub-branding strategy proved to be "a unique differentiator in a market dominated by numbers and cutting-edge codenames"[2]. According to Llyod Mathias, there were several other factors that contributed to Motorola's late but significant growth in India apart from

---

[1] **"Motorola MotoYuva W180 launched in India",** http://news.techwhack.com/6917/motorola-motoyuva-w180/, December 3rd 2007

[2] Sangameshwaran Prasad, "How Motorola captured second spot in Nokia country", http://www.rediff.com/l/money/2007/oct/23moto.htm, October 23rd 2007

meticulous sub-branding strategy and they were stronger distribution, wider product range and effective communication techniques adopted in advertisements. In other words, these formed the various critical elements of brand building for Motorola.

Brand Motorola: A Post-Mortem of its Turnaround Strategy

Motorola as a brand in the mobile handsets market reportedly started on a dismal note in India. Although it was among the first to enter the Indian cellular market, it failed to grab substantial market share. Even after a decade of its existence in India, its market share was found to be 2.6%[3] in 2005. In 2005, when Motorola tried to analyze the reasons for its consistent poor performance, it found that consumers had very little belief in the brand. Apart from that, the brand lacked support from retail, trade and opinion leaders. Further, there were later entrants like Sony Ericsson, Samsung and LG that were gaining in consumer acceptance and recognition vis-à-vis Motorola. The country had 150 million mobile users and the cellular service providers were adding six million subscribers every month.[4] It was thus a huge opportunity which Motorola needed to tap in order to not only sustain but also challenge the dominance of Nokia in India.

Motorola's priorities included enhancing its distribution network, offering a distinct identity to the brand, widening its product portfolio and establishing meaningful collaboration with the cellular service providers. Motorola needed to refocus on its brand building strategies so that consumers trusted the brand and there was significant enhancement in the brand's equity **(Exhibit-I)**.

---

[3] **"How Motorola captured second spot in Nokia country", op.cit.**
[4] **Ibid.**

Exhibit-I

The Various Elements of Brand Building

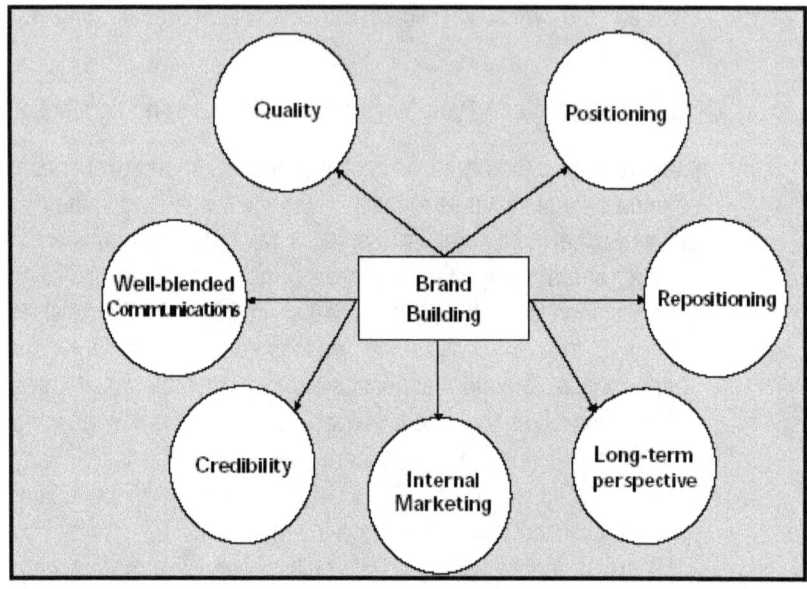

Source:
http://www.tutor2u.net/business/marketing/brands_building_brands.asp

Motorola ensured that all its products were functionally okay and there were no manufacturing defects which actually took care of the quality aspect in the context of brand building. The brand was positioned distinctly vis-à-vis the competition. While other handset makers focused on the features, Motorola focused on the design and style of its phones that immediately was found to. Motorola went for a well conceived repositioning with the objective of wooing the Indian populace. From being known as a company manufacturing products with advanced technology, Motorola became more customer-driven. Products under the umbrella brand Motorola were found to address specific requirements of consumers and there were some products that were designed exclusively for a certain consumer segment. Motorola understood that if it had to survive long-term in the rapidly growing mobile handsets market, it had to establish meaningful collaboration with the retailers and the mobile service providers and accordingly it went for strategic tie-ups to ensure long-term prospects for the brand.

There were certain factors that were found to trigger resurgence for the laggard mobile handset brand. Its thrust on meaningful collaboration with the retailers and mobile service providers, appropriate product development strategies, well-researched communication strategies and most importantly its witty sub-branding strategies were the various reasons that enabled Motorola to gain significant market share in due course of time.

Brand Motorola: Collaborative and Product Development Strategies

With the objective of gaining significant foothold in the mobile handsets market, Motorola was found to collaborate with the retailers as well as with the cellular service providers. In 2005, the company took the first significant step to revamp its distribution when it tied up with its national distributor, Bharti Teletech. The move enabled Motorola to enhance its distribution points from 3000 to 32000 outlets. Motorola handsets were available through various shops-in-shops and multi-brand outlets. With the objective of tapping the rural and semi-urban consumers, Motorola was found to enter into a distribution agreement with ITC's e-choupal division in 2006. The initiative was termed as BharatMoto and its objective was to turn the opinion leaders at the choupals into extensions of Motorola's marketing arm. The mobile handset maker felt that positive word-of mouth generated thus could provide the much needed mileage to the brand. Motorola reportedly opened two exclusive Motostores in Mumbai and Bangalore to provide customers with a suitable platform to experience the entire range of Motorola handsets **(Exhibit-II)**. Commenting on the retail endeavor, Llyod Mathias observed, "With 50 lakh – 60 lakh mobile subscribers added every month and people upgrading their phones frequently, consumers want an enhanced rich retail experience.

This is exactly what Motostore proposes to do."[5] The Motostores displayed the entire range of Motorola phones and accessories and the shops had different sections like the Bluetooth zone, the music zone and had also another section dedicated to entertainment and personalization of phones that offered services to customers like downloading of ringtones, wallpapers and screensavers.

Exhibit-II

A Motostore in India

Source:
http://www.globalgiants.com/archives/fotos/MOTOROLA-ShowroomIndia.jpg

Apart from focusing on retailing, Motorola was found to collaborate with the cellular service providers too. The company tied up with AirTel, Idea, Hutch (now Vodafone) and BSNL to provide low-cost handsets to first time users. The handsets for the above said purpose were priced around INR 1500. Motorola C115 was one such handset that was offered along with new AirTel connections for quite some time **(Exhibit-III)**. The strategy

---

[5] Kannan Swetha, "Motoring Ahead", http://www.thehindubusinessline.com/catalyst/2007/03/15/stories/2007031 500180100.htm, March 15th 2007

offered Motorola several additional outlets apart from its own 30,000 plus distribution points. Expressing his satisfaction on Motorola's collaboration strategy, Llyod Mathias said, "We are today the most preferred partner of cellular operators. We work with most of them – Tata Indicom, AirTel, Idea, Hutch and BSNL."[6]

Exhibit-III

A Snap of Motorola C115

Source: http://www.dancewithshadows.com/tech/images/moto-c115.jpg

As far as product development strategies were concerned, Motorola was found to come up with new models that were sleek in design and with advanced technology. After being stagnant in terms of new product development, Motorola was found to focus actively on launching newer models since 2005 **(Exhibit-IV)**. The Moto RAZR model was created along with its appealing pink

---

[6] **"Motoring Ahead", op.cit.**

colored variant. Moto PBL and Moto SLVR were the other handsets that were launched in end-2005. Moto PBL was launched in six different colors. Motorola had always been found to give emphasis on the glamour quotient of the mobile phones and hence it launched handsets in several colors. One effective strategy that was adopted by Motorola in terms of new product development was that it launched several models in sub- INR 2000 range which eventually was found to be a price point where Nokia dominated in the Indian markets. Motorola launched the Motophone priced at INR 1605 for the smaller towns in India. Commenting on the launch of the Motophone, Llyod Mathias observed, "We are targeting the small towns with the dust-proof and break-free Motophone. It can withstand high temperature and has a clear vision display."[7] Moto Rokr E6 and Moto Ming have been one of Motorola's latest offering in the premium category. Motorola was found to establish its presence in the CDMA category too. It tied up with Tata Indicom to sell its CDMA Razr handsets.

Exhibit-IV

Snaps of Motorola's Handsets

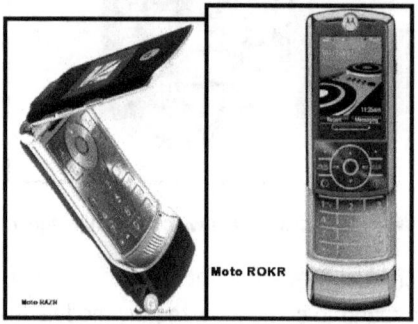

[7] "Motoring Ahead", op.cit.

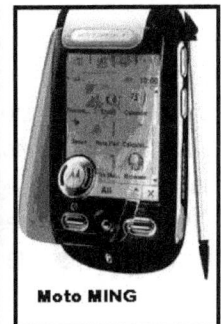

Moto SLVR

Moto MING

Compiled by the author

What's worth noting in the context of new product development strategies adopted by Motorola is that the company has simultaneously launched handsets in both the entry-level as well as in the high-end category. Similar tie-ups have also been reported with Reliance. From just a couple of models Motorola today has around 28 handset models in its stable at various competitive price points.

The collaborative and product development strategies of Motorola were well complemented by some well-researched communication strategies adopted for Brand Motorola.

Communication Strategies

The communication strategy adopted by Motorola was distinctly different from those of its competitors and it was one major reason that heralded the turnaround for Brand Motorola. Motorola's communications were not feature-driven but customer-driven. The campaigns did not highlight much on better color screen, longer battery life or other technical aspects. Rather, they highlighted on the design and the oomph value of the mobile handsets. The basic objective of Motorola's communication strategy was that consumers not just possessed the handsets but also felt tempted to flash them.

The advertisements for Motorola's handsets were thus found to be stylish in their presentation compared to advertisements of competing handsets. Another highlight of Motorola's communication strategy was that they targeted the youth exclusively and were customized as per Indian settings. Motorola found that 80% of the mobile users in the country were mostly first-time buyers in the age bracket of 16-35 years.[8] In other words, the mobile phones category was youth-driven and so Motorola focused its attention on wooing the youth populace through its communication. The content was localized and therefore the ads did not seem to be dubbed versions of its international advertisements. Explaining Motorola's communication strategy, Llyod Mathias opined, "Motorola's communication stands for brand design and coolness. Our communication for India is not a dubbed version of the international ad; our focus is on creating local communication that understands the Indian consumer."[9]

In 2007, for its Moto ROKR E6 model, Motorola was reported to sign Abhishek Bachchan to reinforce its youth propaganda **(Exhibit-V)**. Despite going for celebrity endorsement, Motorola ensured that the product and not the celebrity was the cynosure of the advertisement. The product and its appealing features were well highlighted. It was projected as an addictive material for the youth.

---

[8] **"How Motorola captured second spot in Nokia country", op.cit.**
[9] **"Motoring Ahead", op.cit.**

Exhibit-V

Abhishek Bachchan at the launch of Moto ROKR E6

Source: lh3.google.com/.../cfbMn0u27pg/s800/biz1.jpg

In late 2007, Motorola was found to launch a sub-brand in the name of the youth called Moto YUVA W180 (where YUVA means youth) **(Exhibit-VI)**. The advertisements for the handset reflected the attitudes, tastes and temperaments of today's youth. The handset was promoted with the tagline – "Ab Apni Suno". In other words, Moto YUVA highlighted the fact that today's youth are capable of taking their own decisions and need not be coerced to do certain things by their parents as per their wish. The advertisements for the product were humorous and presented such situations that were quite identifiable with the youth of today.

Exhibit-VI

The Moto YUVA Mobile Phone

Source:
http://www.compareindia.com/media/images/2007/nov/img_30405_motoyu
va_w180.jpg

Apart from the advertising campaigns, Motorola's promotional strategies have involved the Internet to a large extent. Apart from ads on Yahoo!, Motorola was found to develop certain consumer engagement initiatives through the website, *MotoStar.in* which reported to have registered 98,000 users.

Apart from the communication tactics adopted by Motorola, the company's sub-branding strategies enabled it to differentiate Brand Motorola from competing mobile handset brands.

The Sub-branding Strategies

Motorola was found to pursue research-based sub-branding strategies in order to expand its product portfolio. Sub-brands by definition, refers to those subordinate brands that exist under the umbrella of the parent brand. They offer related but significantly different features and benefits compared to the parent brand. Motorola took the initiative of defining the roles of the sub-brand suitably so that a coherent and effective branding system could be established.

Brand Motorola's sub-brands have been found to describe offerings in a very precise manner. In other words, they have communicated the product class, a key feature or function, a target segment well. Examples like FLIP MOTO or FOTO MOTO are such that describe a key function in a particular handset. FLIP MOTO actually referred to the flip phones of Motorola that offer the function of portability while FOTO MOTO referred to the mobile phones with cameras. MP3 MOTO was another example in this context. The recently launched MOTO YUVA describes the key target segment viz. the youth. MOTO has been one word that has been used by Motorola both as a prefix as well as a suffix in its sub-branding strategy. The word has been found to add a new dimension to the sub-brands. Motorola's sub-brands have been found to focus on poorly served market niches in India. There had been some die-hard music lovers who wanted a mobile phone that could be compatible as a portable musical equipment with lots of playing options. Motorola with its MP3 MOTO was successful in serving the above said consumer segment. MOTO RAZR was an example of Motorola's sub-branding strategy that defined the sharp features of the mobile handset in the context of design.

For Motorola, sub-branding was reportedly the best strategy available for expansion as because it offered the company a chance to launch a host of products with distinct identities under the parent brand, Motorola. The role played by the parent brand was that of reassurance- a reassurance to customers that a sub-brand could be well trusted for it was part of the Motorola stable, a reputed name in the international mobile handsets market. A co-driver relationship as well as a driver descriptor relationship was found to exist between the parent brand and the sub-brands. The parent brand Motorola created familiar association while the sub-brand contributed to an imagery that appealed to specific consumer segments. Moreover, the parent brand Motorola provided the basic motivation for consumers to buy the brand while the sub-brand provided a description of a product as a descriptor. The stylish sub-brands like RAZR, FOTO, ROKR along with the word MOTO created a distinct identity for the sub-brands and established them firmly in the consumer's perceptual territory. It added to the recall value of the products. Generally, it had been observed that consumers tend to forget those sub-brand names which are in the form of numbers which is the case with most mobile brands. For example, Nokia has sub-brands like 3310, 3315, 3230 etc. But by going for stylishly short and specific sub-brand names, Motorola was found to hit the bull's eye with its sub-branding strategy.

The above said strategies of Motorola enabled it to acquire the No. 2 slot in terms of market share in mid-2006. Around this time, Motorola's market share climbed to 7.6%[10] and by end-2006, it was 17%[11]. Analysts estimated that Motorola handsets sold over 1.4 million[12] a month in 2007. As per a market research survey conducted in the same year, Motorola's equity with retailers had skipped from 18% to 39%.[13] What's more interesting was the observation that 21% of consumers considered Brand Motorola a cool and trendy mobile handset brand compared to 6% earlier.[14] While summarizing Brand Motorola's efforts to maintain the

---

[10] "How Motorola captured second spot in Nokia country", op.cit.

[11] Anand Sanjay, "The market is talking about a MotoComeback", http://www.financialexpress.com/old/fe_full_story.php?content_id=148074 , December 5th 2006

[12] "How Motorola captured second spot in Nokia country", op.cit.

[13] Ibid.

[14] Ibid.

growth momentum, Suresh Kumar, director, Mindspark Consulting opined, "The recent efforts by Motorola and the launch of a spate of models which are sleek and affordable would strike the right chord with the youth segment that seeks to change their mobile phone every year or so. Abhishek Bachchan as brand ambassador is an excellent fit- the move reinforces Motorola as the choice for the tech-savvy youth. The brand's awareness and visibility has certainly increased for more than one reason- besides celebrity endorsement and heavy advertising in mass media but also the brand's integrated effort in improving their distribution and availability at many more outlets as well as good branding at retail points. To fight competition and gain market share, Motorola has to sustain this momentum generated by new product designs and distinctive communications efforts. Getting into strategic alliances with brands and services that appeal to youth would be a way forward."[15]

---

[15] **"Motoring Ahead", op.cit.**

Annexure II: CASELET

The Wow Spa

The Wow Thai and Aroma Spa was launched in Kolkata in 2011. It not only enjoyed a location advantage in each of its 5 outlets, but also specialized in massages for both men and women. Prior to its launch, The Wow adopted an aggressive promotional strategy. They had print ads, outdoor ads, hoardings, flyers, radio ads, etc. It called itself "Experts in Thai and Aroma Massages".

The ambience of each of the outlets lived up to its brand positioning. The décor was Thai, with soft Thai music in the background. The masseurs and massage therapists were also clothed in Thai outfits. The interiors, lighting and gizmos were dazzling. Any customer who walked in expected the best service, not only because of the promotions, but also because of the ambience of the place. The initial response to their opening was great.

However, problem arose when it was found that the service providers were not as 'expert' in their field as previously claimed. Some of them would even get angry at the customers if they provided suggestions on how they would like a massage. They claimed that the customers didn't know what a real Thai and Aroma massage is and that they need not learn from the customers. Others even complained that they were not getting their money's worth. Several service gaps surfaced very quickly. One of the prominent gap was that the 'People' factor was missing in each of the outlets. Customers who came once did not want to come back a second time.

Annexure III: ARTICLE

Controversies: How They Make or Break Celebrity Brands?

It was widely felt at one point of time that controversies only create a negative impact on the careers of celebrities. It was due to this reason that advertisers often were in a dilemma while going for celebrity endorsements. While on one hand, celebrities assured sufficient awareness about a product/service, there was always a threat that if a celebrity got involved in any sort of controversy, it might well spell a doom for the brand being advertised by the concerned celebrity.

However in recent times, we have come across several instances where controversies have either made a celebrity out of an ordinary individual or it has helped in breathing a new lease of life into the otherwise declining career of a celebrity. Celebrities have successfully leveraged controversies to grab the attention of the media and capture the mindshare of audiences. In other words, in controversies have been increasingly playing a defining role as far as the making of celebrity brands is concerned.

Get Controversial. Get Famous

Across various professional domains, there are instances where an individual has been catapulted to instant and incredible stardom due to a controversy **(Exhibit-I)**. A meteoric rise in name and fame that was perhaps unachievable by the individual. From the world of modern literature, we have Taslima Nasreen who got known to the world only after her book 'Lajja' garnered wrath of the Muslim fundamentalists and they went on to issue *fatwa* against her. In the same vein, we can name Salman Rushdie too. Yes, the gentleman was awarded the *Booker Prize* for his novel, 'The Midnight's Children' but it was his controversial book 'Satanic Verses' that made Rushdie famous as an author in the arena of international modern English literature.

Exhibit-I
Controversies Made Them Famous

Compiled by the author

M.F. Hussain is definitely a great painter of our country but controversies has been mainly responsible to turn this painting maestro into a popular celebrity brand. His constant depiction of Hindu Gods and Goddesses in nude or his passion to paint abstract forms of Bollywood actresses like Madhuri Dixit and Tabu have been the factors that have offered tremendous fame and fan following to the veteran painter.

Among the international celebrities, Paris Hilton is one individual who can safely thank the controversies surrounding her for being a 'hot' celebrity brand today. She featured in a raunchy sex video few years back and that made the world take notice of her and she went on to seek instant stardom. Later, it was the term spent in the country jail for reckless driving that made headlines in the international media. Britney Spears is another personality who has in recent times been more popular due to controversies rather than her career as an international pop sensation. She was involved in the shortest celebrity wedding of all time with Jason Allen Alexander. Her marriage to Jason for 55 hours was one news item that made headlines for a long time. Her subsequent marriage to Kevin Federline and the recording of her childbirth for distribution in the media were some other controversies that assured lots of audience mindshare. In recent times, the tonsuring of her hair, her indecent behavior in the public and being seen often without panties have been some other controversies surrounding the pop diva.

The one Bollywood actress of today who has been largely famous due to controversies is Mallika Sherawat. It has been felt that the actress has made a conscious effort over the years to keep herself embroiled in controversies. Whether it has been her choice of movies, the portrayal of roles in the movies or her interaction in the media, Mallika Sherawat has been undoubtedly controversy's favorite child. Controversies have not just enabled the starlet to seek a strong foothold in the Hindi film industry but have also offered her opportunities to be noticed by the international cine fraternity. Her movie, 'The Myth' with Jackie Chan is one such example. Celebrities have utilized controversies in various other ways to seek fame and greater mileage in their professional domains.

Victims of Controversy
Many times, a controversy involves two individuals. One of them happens to be the cause of the controversy while the other is the victim of the controversy. It has been observed that often a victim of a controversy not only generates huge amount of sympathy

but also the controversy helps a budding or an established celebrity to gain greater mileage in his/her career. The controversy involving Danielle Llyod and Shilpa Shetty in the international reality show, *Celebrity Big Brother* is an example to be stated over here. The racism comments made by Llyod about Shetty sparked off significant protests in India and abroad and generated tremendous amount of sympathy wave for Shetty. Such was the effect of the controversy that Shilpa Shetty was found to win the contest comfortably. Not just that, the controversy turned the Indian actress into an international celebrity and she went on to promote her own range of perfume called *S2*. The controversy and her subsequent win gave a new lease of life to Shetty's Bollywood career.

Rakhi Sawant was hardly known to many people while she was doing item numbers in movies and doing some indecent moves in private videos until the Mika 'kiss controversy' happened. It was alleged that the Punjabi pop singer, Mika had forcibly tried to kiss Rakhi at a birthday party and thus outraged her modesty. The case was seriously taken up by women groups who portrayed Rakhi Sawant as a victim of sexual harassment. Like Shetty, Rakhi Sawant was beamed over various news channels where she was found to share her ignoble experience and her helplessness. The controversy not only made Rakhi Sawant a household name but it also seemed to boost her professional career as a dancer. She participated in the reality show 'Nach Baliye' and was also featured in various other reality shows. Rakhi Sawant has been someone who has utilized the 'victimized' tool to good effect **(Exhibit-II)**. In 'Nach Baliye', she proclaimed that Star Plus had wrongly denied her from winning the contest. Recently, she had similar things to share about her item song in the movie 'Krazzy 4' where she said that the song was wrongly deleted before the release of the movie.

Exhibit-II
Leveraging on the 'Victimized' Tag

Compiled by the author

However, controversies might not always do good to a celebrity as far as his professional career is concerned.

The Flip Side

Controversies have often impacted celebrity brands in a negative way also (Exhibit-III). The case of Tom Cruise is an example.

Tom Cruise was a popular actor and high brand worth celebrity of Hollywood before controversies surrounded him for his open support of *Scientology*, his comments regarding anti-depressant drugs, his relationship and subsequent marriage to Katie Holmes and his infamous actions in the *Oprah Winfrey Show*. Controversy had a telling effect on the box-office prospect of Cruise's movie, Mission Impossible III. It was the controversy risk associated with Cruise that prompted Sumner Redstone owned Paramount Pictures to sever its professional ties with the Cruise-Wagner Productions owned by Tom Cruise. After Cruise joined hands with United Artists, the movie production house had similar apprehensions about the movies being produced by United Artists featuring Tom Cruise as lead actor.

In the context of Bollywood, Sunjay Dutt's alleged involvement in the Mumbai blast case and Salman Khan's involvement in the black buck case and the 'hit and run' case (where a pedestrian was killed in the incident) were instances where these actors' popularity and acceptance among the cine goers was negatively impacted. Salman Khan lost the acceptability and the 'craze factor' that was existent among the female cine goers prior to the occurrence of the above mentioned controversies. Although Sunjay Dutt received several accolades for the portrayal of the celluloid character 'Munna Bhai', the blemish on his personality continued to exist. Mohammed Azharuddin was one of the most successful Indian cricket skippers and commanded huge fan following for his incredible wrist work while batting but once the match-fixing controversy happened and Azharuddin was found involved in the matter, he not only lost his fan base but also his chances of being a cricket commentator post retirement.

Exhibit-III
The Negative Impact of Controversies

Compiled by the author

Controversies arise when there is a gap between the actual and perceived image of a celebrity brand. Controversies do give rise to curiosity about a celebrity brand. At times, it works in favor of a celebrity while at other times; it taints the career of the celebrity and leaves an indelible mark. Frankly speaking, controversy is a coin comprising two opposite outcomes. It is the work of the media, audience psyche and the luck factor of the celebrity that defines the outcome once the controversy coin concerning a celebrity gets tossed. An effective way to confront controversies however is to come upfront and tackle the problem head-on with utmost integrity. Recognizing the problem and taking relevant corrective action is a tried and tested method to bail oneself out of controversies.

References:

- http://en.wikipedia.org

- Chowdary Asha, "Brand me now!", *The Times of India (Times Life!),* March 9th 2008

About the Author

Kisholoy Roy is an Accredited Management Teacher who has several years of experience in the industry and academics. He is presently pursuing his PhD from Indian School of Mines, Dhanbad. He has several publications to his credit that includes text books, case studies, articles and research papers. Over the years as a teacher he has been actively pursuing case based education which his students have thoroughly liked and that has propelled him to be an extremely popular faculty among students. In this book, he has shared many of his experiences related to case based teaching and case writing.